OTHER TITLES OF INTEREST FROM ST

The Motivating Team Leader

The Skills of Encouragement: Bringing Out the Best in

What Is, Is: Encouraging Yourself to Accept What
Change What You Can

Real Dream
Achieve Extr

Leadership b

Organization

Team Buildin

The New Leader: Bringing kplace

Reengineering the Training Function: How to Align Training with the New Corporate Agenda

Teams in Government: A Handbook for Team-Based Organizations

Mastering the Diversity Challenge: Easy On-the-Job Applications for Measurable Results

For more information about these titles call, fax or write:

St. Lucie Press
100 E. Linton Blvd., Suite 403B
Delray Beach, FL 33483
TEL (561) 274-9906 • FAX (561) 274-9927

StL

Best Team Skills

50 Key Skills for Unlimited Team Achievement

Best Team Skills

Dr. Lewis E. Losoncy

St. Lucie Press
Delray Beach, Florida

Printed and bound in the U.S.A. Printed on acid-free paper.
10 9 8 7 6 5 4 3 2 1

ISBN 1-57444-085-3

Direct all inquiries to St. Lucie Press, Inc., 100 E. Linton Blvd., Suite 403B, Delray Beach, Florida 33483.

Phone: (561) 274-9906
Fax: (561) 274-9927

StL

Published by
St. Lucie Press
100 E. Linton Blvd., Suite 403B
Delray Beach, FL 33483

With love, to my teammates—

My wife, Diane, our center

Gabrielle Losoncy, our energy

Tyler Baker, our athlete

Lauren Losoncy, a symbol of understanding

Amy Oxenrider, our writer

Eric Oxenrider, our builder

and the team at St. Lucie Press, our competence

CONTENTS

The Seven Principles of Mutual Encouragement to Turn Individuals into an Encouraging Winning Team

PHASE I—SYNERGY
Focus on Feelings

PHASE II—EXPANDING THE MATRIX OF OUR MINDS
Focus on Thinking

PREFACE

"That'll never work!" shouts the burly manager. "We tried that before and we almost lost our shirts."

"Any other suggestions?" the manager continues.

All is quiet on this team.

Have you been on a team like this? Amazingly, the most consequential influence on a team's success or failure is the team members' skills to encourage—or lack of skills, which often may even discourage others. Curiously, most teams are thrown together without any encouragement skill training to build an effective team by bringing out the best in others. We create teams to produce a synergy of results unreachable by individuals alone. So why stack the odds against our team's success by not offering people the skills to encourage their teammates?

With the ***best*** (***b***ecoming an ***e***ncouraging ***s***uccess ***t***eam) team skills, teams quickly move beyond floundering in inefficient, ineffective and discouraging communications and struggling with personal agendas, egos, competitiveness, cliquishness and even apathy. Just as there are vital technical skills that team members need in their own areas of expertise, there are consequential team skills that are necessary to build responsible, involved, committed team players. Based on the seven principles of mutual encouragement—*synergy, cooperation, focus, respect, reality, optimism* and *progress*—the fifty best team skills will make your team members encouragers. Each mutual encouragement skill is defined and then acquired through over one hundred encouragement opportunity exercises throughout the book. Each mutual encouragement skill is then reinforced with a few key thoughts.

The best team skills can be used to (1) help you become a more encouraging team member with your work team, family team or sports team or (2) help your whole team acquire the skills to become mutual encouragers. The skills can be learned through self-instruction or group instruction. Each skill is presented in an easy-to-read format and can be learned and incorporated in a quick manner to move your team onward through *synergy, cooperation, focus, respect, reality, optimism* and *progress* to reach your unlimited dreams—together.

Guarantee the next team you are on works. Build the *best* team!

ABOUT THE AUTHOR

Dr. Lewis E. Losoncy is a psychologist and the author of fourteen books on encouragement, success, leadership and teamwork, including *The Motivating Team Leader* and *The Skills of Encouragement.*

Dr. Losoncy is responsible for building an encouragement team at Matrix Essentials (Solon, Ohio), North America's largest manufacturer of professional-only beauty products.

He has appeared on numerous TV and radio programs, including CNN and CBS's "This Morning," and has been featured in assorted print media, from *The Wall Street Journal* to *Psychology Today.*

Dr. Losoncy has lectured in all fifty states, most of the Canadian provinces, and throughout Australia and New Zealand.

TEAMWORK MAKES THE DREAM WORK

"A Team's Source of Motivation Is One Shared Dream. When You Share a Dream Together, You Become a Team!"

Is Our Team a Bunch of Individuals or an Encouraging Winning Team?

The difference between a bunch of individuals and an encouraging team is increased cooperation, involvement, productivity and synergy:

A Bunch of Individuals	*An Encouraging Winning Team*
1 + 1 + 1 + 1 + 1 = 5	1 × 2 × 3 × 4 × 5 = 120

The science of team dynamics has shown that the whole team will produce either more or less than a bunch of individuals will produce alone, depending upon the way the individual parts of the team work together. Team synergy is the bonus that is achieved when all parts of a team encourage each other to work together to achieve their shared dream.

Winning teams rarely happen by chance or luck. Winning teams are the result of the commitment of individuals to rise above their own self-interest or cliquish interest and become mutual encouragers. The collective spirit of encouraging winning teams is experienced when each teammate actually lives the seven principles of mutual encouragement. If every teammate makes this commitment to bring out the best in others, each teammate will, almost immediately, begin the most fulfilling journey of his or her professional life. And, most importantly, they won't be alone.

Benefits of Becoming an Encouraging Winning Teammate

The best team skills is a positive and practical approach to developing the skills to motivate yourself and others. By understanding the seven principles of mutual encouragement, your team can create its own (1) synergy, (2) cooperation, (3) determined focus, (4) mutual respect, (5) reality base, (6) optimism and (7) progress. An encouraging winning team with team synergy offers many more benefits to everyone because:

- An encouraging winning team helps you realize your important role in contributing to your best team's dream.
- An encouraging winning team is united by sharing a common dream.
- An encouraging winning team helps instill not only individual pride, but pride in being a part of the team as well.
- An encouraging winning team leads to greater mutual respect because it increases the value of each teammate's role in the success of the team.
- An encouraging winning team brings your team closer by emphasizing cooperation over competition.
- An encouraging winning team plays a major role in fulfilling your social and emotional needs, leading to greater

well-being, happiness and fulfillment. In addition, the encouragement you receive from others increases your morale, motivation, creativity and involvement. And you will have the skills to encourage your teammates to feel the same way.

Learning the best team skills also gives you a fringe benefit. These encouragement skills will be beneficial in your family and social life as well.

The Seven Principles of Mutual Encouragement to Turn Individuals into an Encouraging Winning Team

Phase I: Synergy—Focus on Feelings

Principle 1—The Synergy Principle

"All of Us Together Can Do More
Than Each of Us Can Do Alone"

Invitation skills • Warmth skills • Sensitive-listening skills • Empathic-responding skills • Questioning skills • Personalizing skills • Enthusiasm skills • Agreement skills • Mutuality skills • Positioning skills • Accessibility skills • Sensory-representational skills

Principle 2—The Cooperation Principle

"Competing Divides Us;
Cooperating Multiplies Us"

Social-interest skills • Cooperative-listening skills • Credibility skills • Universalizing skills • Genuineness skills • Mutual-reliance skills • Conflict-resolution skills

Phase II: Expanding the Matrix of Our Minds—Focus on Thinking

Principle 3—The Focus Principle

"Determining Our Destination
Determines Our Destiny"

Shared-vision skills • Mutual-determinism skills • Anticipation skills • Choosing skills • Self-starting skills • Goal-centering skills

Principle 4—The Respect Principle

"Centering on Each Other's Strengths Builds Our Force"

Self-encouragement skills • Asset-focusing skills • Liability-into-asset skills • Relating-individual-assets-to-team-goal skills • Respecting skills • Expectation skills

Principle 5—The Reality Principle

"Accepting 'What Is' Is Our Only Real Starting Point"

Objectivity skills • Acceptance skills • Humor skills • Relabeling skills • Rational-thinking skills • Assertiveness skills • Welcoming-criticism skills

Principle 6—The Optimism Principle

"Believing Problems Have Solutions Gives Us the Advantage"

Overcoming-discouraging-belief skills • Certainty skills • Find-a-way skills • Perceptual-alternative skills • Optimistic-explanatory skills

Phase III: Action and Progress—*Focus on Doing*

Principle 7—The Progress Principle

"Encouraging Progress Precedes Praising Success"

Becoming skills • Effort-focusing skills • Spotting-improvement skills • Contribution-recognition skills • Evaluating-action skills • Credit-sharing skills • Celebration skills

Encouragement: The Key to Building the Best Team

Study teams of people. Any team. A sports team. A family unit. The team of people in a company. In fact, observe any time two or more people are united for some common purpose. The goal could be to win together, to overcome an obstacle together or even to achieve a dream together, whether it be landing a teammate on the moon or increasing customer satisfaction.

Observe how the individuals on the team work, move, flow

and interact together. Experience how they feel and care about each other. Sense whether they discourage and ignore or they encourage and support one another. Make mental notes about the attitudes and skills of the team members who encourage others. These catalysts add to the team's total force by bringing out the best in each person.

Watch a high school basketball team move down the court together. Spot patterns of interaction. Look for the synergy. Feel the motion between the players. Does each team member know where the others are? Or does one pass the ball to an empty space? Does each teammate act as if he or she believes it is important to encourage the teammate who misses an important shot? Or do some players think that you pick the team up by putting a teammate down? Are the team members so bogged down by struggles and internal competition that they forget who their real opponent is—the other team?

What about your team? Do you feel your team flows as one? Is each person there to encourage others to reach higher performance levels? Do you feel a part of the unity? Could you be more productive with additional encouragement from your teammates? Do you think each of your teammates could be more productive with encouragement from you? Could your own extra effort to encourage actually make a difference to the team? You can bet on it!

Why do some teams have just the right chemistry and work together, experiencing fulfillment while reaching their goals? Why do other teams, caught up in their own inner strife and lack of unity, never gel as a unit? Is a winning team the result of luck? Or is a winning team the result of deliberate planning and design?

The motivating difference between winning and losing teams is encouragement. Winning teams are filled with people who recognize the opportunity to be a positive force. Encouragers recognize that their own encouragement can influence their teammates' morale, attitude, fun and progress.

How does encouragement work to produce a winning team? Your personal experience may already have shown you that it is almost impossible for a team of discouragers to defeat a team of encouraging people. Why does an encouraging team produce dramatically more positive results than a discouraging team? A team of encouragers uses the power of people synergy.

The Best Teams Include, Rather Than Exclude, Teammates

A discouraging team is characterized by isolation, selfishness and cliques. Energies are used to exclude others rather than to include them and their thoughts and contributions. The atmosphere on a discouraging team is one of bits and pieces, separate individuals and groups. There is an absence of total team synergy. In addition, when a new person joins a discouraging team, cliques are slow to warm up to the new teammate.

On the best teams, encouraging teammates rise above their own self-interest and the interests of cliques by recognizing the importance of including everyone's ideas. The best teams become more fully functioning. The added benefit of everyone working together harmoniously is what synergy is all about.

The goal of the mutual encouragement process is to inspire everyone on the team with a winning, working together attitude by developing their skills to bring out the best in each other. The following attitudinal and behavioral directions will occur on your team as a result of mutual encouragement.

DISCOURAGING TEAM *Excludes (–)*	*ENCOURAGING TEAM* *Synergizes (+)*
From	To
Shuts out, closed	Lets in, open
Judgmental	Seeks to understand
Fearful, protective	Courageous, enriched
Focuses on negative outcomes of including	Focuses on enlarging and growing together by understanding each other's team roles

DISCOURAGING TEAM *Excludes (–)*	*ENCOURAGING TEAM* *Synergizes (+)*
Dwells on one's own pressures	Moves to understand pressures on other teammates
Sees only my own world	Uses perceptual alternatives to get a team view
Exclusionary tactics: (1) Denial (2) Dehumanizing or distancing (3) Discrediting source of idea	Inclusionary approaches: (1) Openness (2) Rehumanizing (3) Recognizes that the value of an idea is based upon the value of the idea, not the source
Motivated by maintaining the status quo	Motivated by desire to grow, intelligent enough to take a new perspective and stable enough to see possible limitations of current view
Emphasizes differences, ignores similarities (e.g., same team)	Emphasizes similarities, values differences as a source to enrich the team
Builds walls	Builds doors and windows
Denies or heightens conflicts	Initiates process to resolve conflicts

The Best Teams Cooperate Rather than Compete with Teammates

On a discouraging team, people compete with each other ("It's you versus me"). The underlying thinking is, "If you perform better than me, that means I am less of a person than you. So, if we are in competition with each other, I don't want you to succeed. It makes me feel big when you aren't doing well. I have to do everything I can to put you down as a way of picking myself up."

The team won't go very far when it is moved by a negative motivation directed against each other rather than toward the real competition, which is achieving the team's goals.

The best team proceeds in the spirit of cooperation with other teammates. Encouragers know that the better each person performs, the better the team does. The better the team does, the better I, as a teammate, will do. Doesn't it make sense that cooperation achieves so much more unity than competing? Sense the differences between teammates who compete versus those who cooperate.

COMPETES (–)	*COOPERATES (+)*
Uncooperative stance	Sees opportunity in unity
Listens competitively when others speak	Listens to learn and combine
Listens to divide	Listens to synergize views
Outdoing mindset, plays one-upmanship	Cooperation mindset
My way	Our way
Moves away or against	Moves with
Winner/loser mentality	Mutual winner mentality
Others are guilty until proven innocent	Proceeds with trust
Plays games, manipulative	Builds credibility and is trustworthy

The Best Teams Have a Mutually Determined Shared Focus

Discouraging teams are composed of isolated individuals or cliques with no unified, collective purpose. Lacking a shared focus, discouraging teams are motivated and determined by chance, luck and wishes rather than by mutually determined conscious choice. Because of their lack of unity, discouraging teams have very little synergy. The feeling is, "You do your thing. What you do has no effect on me." For example, "If this customer isn't mine, then I don't have to be nice to her. That's somebody else's job."

Encouraging teams have their eyes and hearts focused on the shared dream. Each person knows not only his or her own role, but also the team's ultimate focus. The team's dream is bigger than any individual. Encouraging teams also believe in mutual determination. "Our outcome is determined by us, not by things outside our control. Together we determine our destination." They feel self-assured because they know what they are going to achieve. They know it is up to them and they can do it. They are unified by a common purpose. "If I am nice to this customer, even though he is not mine, he'll be back and our whole business will progress." The laser-like focus on a shared purpose creates synergy. Synergy is the bonus that is earned by working together harmoniously. It moves the team closer to the dream.

The best teams get a powerful boost from synergy by having a common direction and goal. Consider the differences between a helpless team with no control over its future and a focused team.

AIMLESS *Externally Determined (–)*	*FOCUSED* *Mutually Determined (+)*
Thinks "just get by"	Thinks "bigger and better"
No standards or low standards	Constantly raising standards
Pointless, no destination	Laser-like aim at a goal, destined to hit higher target
Limited vision	Visualizes achievement of goal
Pushed by fear	Pulled by power of goal
Pain avoiding ("I'll do my part so I won't get into trouble")	Pleasure seeking, and achieving can be pleasurable
Haphazard movement, no direction or plan, determined by chance	Organized, predetermined plan set up by team

AIMLESS *Externally Determined (–)*	*FOCUSED* *Mutually Determined (+)*
No anticipation of problems, energies consumed by crises	Problems solved up front, energies involved in creativity
Easily distracted	Rock-like focus on goal
Other-directed	Self-directed
Extrinsic motivation	Intrinsic motivation
Stimulus-response: "We are helpless products of external happenings"	Stimulus-*we*-response: "We choose our response to our environment"
Environmentally determined future	Mutually determined future
"We are the effects of things in the environment"	"We are the cause of things that affect our environment"
Excuses, dwells on what's missing	"We have an abundance of resources contained within our team"
"Who is going to motivate me?"	"The momentum starts here!"

The Best Teams Center on What's Right with Each Other

Discouraging teams constantly dwell on shortcomings and mistakes. Teammates are quick to spot what's wrong with each other.

The best teams spotlight the unique positive strengths, assets and resources in each teammate. Plus, encouragers have faith in each other. They constantly communicate, "I believe in you. You can do it!" Don't you perform at higher levels when you are inspired by people who believe in you? Encouraging teams build winners who are motivated by an awareness of how they can use their assets, strengths and resources to make their community a more upbeat place. Sense the difference between focusing on what's right rather than what's wrong with each other.

LIMITATIONS CENTERED (–)	*RESPECT CENTERED (+)*
Centers on mistakes	Highlights positive actions
Quick to see what's wrong ("We missed 5% of our goals")	Spotlights what's right with self and others ("We reached 95% of our goals")
Reinforces weaknesses	Reinforces strengths
Destroys and puts down	Constructs and builds up teammates
Identifies liabilities	Identifies greatest assets
Uses liabilities to show why the team can't	Focuses on the team's assets to convince the team why they can
Sees potential limited by past performance	Sees hidden resources in self and others
Literal	Possibility thinking
Dull and uninvolved	Enthusiastic about the team's potential
Doubts	"I believe in us!"
Disrespects self or others ("Let me do your job for you" or "Do my job for me because I can't")	Communicates respect ("We can do it" or "We have the resources on our team to get this job done" or "Let's show the world what we are made of")
Defeatist team talk	Positive team talk
Negative expectations	High, positive expectations

The Best Teams Face Difficult Realities Together

Discouragers are their own worst enemies. They frustrate themselves by taking setbacks, whether late clients, difficult people, or even traffic jams and the weather, personally. They spend much of their energy unproductively. Discouragers complain about things rather than dealing with them to improve their team.

Individuals on encouraging teams start off with the facts. They have a healthy realization that "what is, is" rather than complaining about their personal "should be's."

They ask themselves whether or not something can be changed. If they believe something can't be changed, they simply accept it—pure and simple—and move on to the next issue.

As a result, the best teams aren't frustrated by setbacks. Encouragers help each other to find humor by viewing setbacks as mere inconveniences and challenges. In an encouraging, humor-filled, lightened atmosphere, every person on the team is more likely to laugh at life's little inconveniences. Realize the difference between a team that wastes its energies focusing on what should have been rather than "what is."

OUT OF TOUCH WITH REALITY (–)	*REALITY IS STARTING POINT (+)*
Frustrating view of reality	Productive view of reality
Reality is "what I would like, what I wish would be, what should be, what ought to be, what must be, what could be, what would be if..., what used to be, things should be easier," etc.	"What is, is!"
Complains about the facts	Accepts the facts
Blames reality	Takes responsibility to change what can be changed
Ignores obstacles	Recognizes and faces obstacles
Twists or distorts "what is" ("It will be easy to land on the moon")	Accepts reality ("This will be tough, but we can handle it")

OUT OF TOUCH WITH REALITY (–)	*REALITY IS STARTING POINT (+)*
Delusions (false beliefs)	Clear perception of reality
Acts without anticipating results	Realizes actions have consequences
Irrational thinking	Rational thinking
Crisis as devastating	Crisis as opportunity
Makes setbacks worse	Sees situation and seeks solution
Catastrophizes setbacks	Faces setbacks and deals with them
Exaggerated self-talk ("This is horrible, terrible—just awful")	Realistic self-talk ("This is just an inconvenience")
Overwhelmed	Motivated to solve problems
Tries to get others to join in on "pity us" party	Motivates others to overcome obstacles
Spends energy making excuses	Spends energy accepting what can't be changed, then changes what can be

The Best Teams Proceed as If Problems Have Solutions

Discouraging teams have an odor of pessimism about them. When given the opportunity to raise their standards and set new goals, they consume all their energies finding explanations why they can't.

The best teams employ less energy when facing a barrier by using their unlimited, creative determination to find a way over the barrier. The major advantage an optimistic synergy success team has is its underlying belief that all problems have solutions. Contrast the difference between pessimistic and optimistic teams.

PESSIMISTIC (–)	*OPTIMISTIC, CREATIVE (+)*
Uses the power of negative belief to work against progress ("It'll never work" or "It's impossible")	Uses the power of positive belief to work for progress ("We can do it" or "Let's find a way")
"Problems are overwhelming"	"Problems have solutions"
"Unless we are perfect, we are worthless"	"Partial solutions are a start"
Moves forward unconvinced	Moves forward with certainty
Negative explanatory style: explains setbacks as (1) personal, (2) permanent and (3) pervasive	Positive explanatory style: explains setbacks as (1) related to an event, (2) temporary and (3) do not affect any other area in life
Explains achievements as (1) luck, (2) temporary and (3) do not affect any other area in life	Explains achievements as (1) personal, (2) permanent and (3) ability to do anything
Focuses on ego, self-conscious	Focuses on results, stays targeted on the mission
Emphasis on equating human worth with performance ("I'm a rotten person because I messed up")	Emphasis on evaluating the task ("We need to make some corrections")
Limits problem solving to conscious mind ("I don't have an immediate answer to the problem, so there probably is no solution")	Uses powers of subconscious, creative mind to find a way ("Somewhere in the universe of my mind there is a solution to the problem in front of us")

The Best Teams Emphasize Effort, Improvement and Progress

Discouraging teams dwell on success and failure. Often the fear of failure holds back their creativity and their willingness to accept change. Teammates fear trying new things because of the overemphasis on success and failure. Discouraged people quickly learn never to do anything that they might not do perfectly.

In contrast, encouraging teams notice and reinforce each other's efforts to stretch, improve, learn and progress. By focusing on effort, everyone is encouraged to grow because progress is viewed as the first step toward success. Aren't you more willing to try when you are among encouragers who focus on helping you grow and emphasize the importance of self-improvement?

After understanding these and many other reasons why the best teams win while discouraging teams lose, it's hard to imagine why organizations don't spend more time building teams that work and win together. Experience the difference between a team that only watches success or failure and one that values progress.

DISCOURAGES (–)	*ENCOURAGES EFFORT, IMPROVEMENT AND PROGRESS (+)*
Focuses only on success and failure	Focuses on progress
Completed jobs are the only things that count	Effort and improvement valued as important
Perfection is more important than growth (results in a non-creative, limiting atmosphere)	Progress is more important than perfection (encourages creativity and forward movement)
"Don't do anything you can't do perfectly"	"Have the courage to learn new skills, recognizing that you may not do them perfectly the first time but each time you will improve"
"Only sell to those who you are sure will buy"	"Sell to everyone—you'll learn each time"
Stays in comfort zone	Keeps expanding comfort zone

If the Team Succeeds, So Do You

Teammates, like marriage mates, are "for better or for worse." But teammates, unlike marriage mates, usually do not choose each other. Teammates arrive on the scene at different times from various backgrounds and dissimilar cultures, sometimes speaking divergent languages, as well as having unique training and skills, separate personalities, assorted levels of motivation and distinctly personal needs.

Each unique, self-centered individual (who, being human, might suspect the world revolves around him or her) is brought together under one small umbrella called "the team." Despite everyone having a different personality and assuming different responsibilities, each individual has to cooperate if the team is ever going to fulfill its potential.

If one out of three marriages doesn't work and a marriage involves only two people who are usually from similar backgrounds and who have willingly chosen each other, can you imagine what a monumental task it is to build a winning team?

Only one team wins the World Series. The best team is always the one where everyone chooses at some point to rise above self-interest and make a commitment to the team's dream. This leap involves a higher-level view of what is best for everyone. You'll have a vantage point with the vision that understands that the only way we can become part of a winning team is if we encourage everyone on our team to give it his or her best. Unfortunately, most people never make the simple connection between (1) the more I rise above my self-interest and encourage the team to grow, (2) the more I will grow as a teammate.

The Best Teams Believe Encouragement Is Everyone's Business

Work is a mental–physical–technical experience done in a social and, at times, even an emotional setting. The major reason why people are discouraged at work is not physical fatigue, strain, technical inability or lack of skill. The major source of stress is social. Job stress means feeling stressed around people. When we experience stress around people, we become discouraged at work. Discouragement is the feeling of being alone and not being included as a part of the team. Discouragement is also the result of feeling put down rather than respected and lifted up by others around us. Every discouraged teammate takes away from the team's total potential and hurts every other teammate. A winning team cannot afford even one discouraged member.

We are trained and prepared mentally, physically and technically for our work, but we receive no training in understanding, motivating and encouraging each other. Teamwork is a social, motivational and communicative commitment. Isn't it true that others around us can make our time for better or for worse?

When you boil it down, job stress is basically people stress. But job fulfillment is winning by working together—achieving things together with other people. Our highs and lows in the work environment are related to people. Work is as much a social–emotional–motivational experience as it is a mental–physical–technical experience.

Every team that has won the Super Bowl has won because of each teammate's unselfish and unbending commitment to a unified dream. This involves their respect for each other and their shared desire to encourage each other by seeing what is right in each team member. The best teams choose to make their moment in time together "for better." The loser, which cannot even be called a team, is made up of individuals who decide to work like isolated islands. They are only concerned about self and only focused on what is wrong with the others. Their time together is "for worse."

Most people agree that it is important to keep morale high on a team. Most agree that encouragement is the way to achieve that end. Most of us know that encouragement brings out better, more creative ideas for improvement, while increasing a sense of belonging, team pride and productivity. Most people want to work in an encouraging atmosphere. Even though we understand the importance of encouragement, most of us believe that "others," whether managers, supervisors or the owner, should be the encouragers. Few people ever rise above that view to realize that "I" can make the difference by encouraging others, even the managers, supervisors and owner. "I" can make our workplace a more positive and productive place to be.

Creating an encouraging atmosphere on the team is everyone's business—at all levels. Then, the benefits of encouragement are enjoyed by everyone—at all levels. As an encourager, you are the difference!

Encouragement doesn't happen by chance. Encouragement happens when each member of the team realizes that he or she is important—and also realizes that people in other positions are just as important. Make a commitment not only to do your own job well, but to bring out the best in others. That's encouragement. When people do this for each other, it is mutual encouragement. Just as you have learned the technical aspects of your job, you can learn the principles of encouraging yourself and others to higher levels of achievement.

The people with whom you work are your teammates—and you are theirs. Together your relationship will be "for better or for worse." Make it work. Become the best team by becoming mutual encouragers.

Encouragement starts with you. You are the difference on your synergy success team!

The Best Teams Start with Mutual Encouragement Training

Make a commitment to commit your team to this training program. Then develop one skill at a time with your team. You'll see change almost immediately. Develop your most important resource, your teammates, to bring out the best in each other.

You are just one person, but you can use these same skills to become an encourager to your team, to your family members and to yourself.

Phase I
SYNERGY

Focus on Feelings

Principle 1
THE SYNERGY PRINCIPLE

"All of Us Together Can Do More Than Each of Us Can Do Alone"

Invitation skills

Warmth skills

Sensitive-listening skills

Empathic-responding skills

Questioning skills

Personalizing skills

Enthusiasm skills

Agreement skills

Mutuality skills

Positioning skills

Accessibility skills

Sensory-representational skills

SYNERGY SKILLS

USE OF THIS PARTICULAR SKILL	*INVITES THIS FEELING IN OTHERS*
1. Invitation skills	"I feel welcomed to the team."
2. Warmth skills	"I feel comfortable on this team."
3. Sensitive-listening skills	"I feel accepted."
4. Empathic-responding skills	"I feel understood."
5. Questioning skills	"I feel important."
6. Personalizing skills	"I feel special."
7. Enthusiasm skills	"I feel energized."
8. Agreement skills	"I feel united."
9. Mutuality skills	"I feel connected."
10. Positioning skills	"I feel secure."
11. Accessibility skills	"I feel reassured."
12. Sensory-representational skills	"I feel in harmony with the team."

BEST TEAM SKILL #1—*INVITATION SKILLS*

Invitation skills are those skills that welcome others to the team. Invitation skills "invite" others to experience themselves as a part of the team. They are designed to be used with anyone who joins the team or anyone you think may not feel a part of the team.

Invitation skills include creating visual, auditory and tactile connections.

1. Making eye contact (visual).
2. Smiling while looking at the person (visual).
3. Introducing yourself while shaking hands (auditory and tactile).
4. Asking the person's name, if not known (auditory).
5. Welcoming, using the person's name (e.g., "We're glad to have you on our team, Jim") (auditory).
6. Simply asking again if you don't hear or if you forget the person's name.
7. Showing you are genuinely interested.

Encouragement Opportunity 1—*Welcoming with invitation skills*

A new person joins the team and sits off in the corner by herself. The rest of the teammates are talking to each other, laughing and having fun. Someone tells you that the new person seems stuck up because she doesn't even bother looking at anyone. Some team members think she probably doesn't want to belong. What other possible feelings might she have? How could you use invitation skills to help this new teammate feel welcome?

____

____

____

____

Encouragement Opportunity 2

You are on a team of over thirty people, but you usually work with just five others. The team members have formed cliques and, in many instances, do not even know the names of those outside their clique. Using invitation skills, what could you do to help create more total team synergy?

____

____

____

____

Key Points on Invitation Skills

1. Immediately welcome new teammates with invitation skills.
2. Today, get to know some current teammates who you don't know that well.

BEST TEAM SKILL #2—*WARMTH SKILLS*

Warmth skills are the non-verbal and verbal skills that communicate your caring for your teammates. Your warmth skills help other people feel comfortable and safe with you and, eventually, with the team.

Warmth skills include:

1. Centering on the other person's interests and concerns.
2. Communicating involvement through your facial expressions to show that you are in tune with the moment-to-moment ideas and feelings of the other person (laughing with the other person or showing concern when he or she expresses anxiety).
3. Demonstrating open body language (leaning forward, open arms, smiling face).
4. Being easy to be with.
5. Blocking out all other distractions when the other person speaks.

Encouragement Opportunity 3—*Helping others feel comfortable through your warmth skills*

After introducing yourself to your new teammate, he looks down and says his name very quietly to you. You can barely hear him. He appears very uncomfortable. How could you use warmth skills to help him feel more relaxed?

____

____

____

____

____

Encouragement Opportunity 4

As a person with warmth skills, you would like to help every person on the team feel safe and comfortable. Can you think of some people who you can help? When will you have the opportunity to communicate your interest and caring for them as teammates?

____

____

____

____

____

Key Points on Warmth Skills

1. Immediately become a safe person with new teammates.
2. Use your warmth skills with current teammates who may not feel comfortable with the team.

BEST TEAM SKILL #3—*SENSITIVE-LISTENING SKILLS*

Sensitive-listening skills are the skills of accurately sensing and accepting the perspective of the other person—as he or she sees it. (It is important to note that sensing and accepting do not necessarily mean agreeing. You can sense and accept and disagree.) Sensitive-listening skills, used in the early part of the relationship, are designed to understand the other person's view without interference of your own view.

Sensitive listening occurs when you listen to accept another person's view without the obstruction of your own need to judge, criticize, moralize, advise or appear to "know it all." Sensitive listening involves simply listening to accept how the other person sees things.

Sensitive-listening skills include:

1. Using non-judgmental listening.
2. Listening to grasp the facts in the real world of the other person without interference or advising.
3. Accepting the responsibilities, pressures and frustrations, as well as the joy and pride, in the other person's experiences (for example, knowing the details of his or her job).
4. Communicating acceptance of the other person's world of responsibilities, pressures and frustrations.
5. Hearing things the first time they are said.

Encouragement Opportunity 5—*Acceptance through sensitive-listening skills*

Think of someone on the team with whom you totally disagree on an issue. Using your sensitive-listening skills, listen to the person to understand the way he or she sees the issue.

Tell yourself that you have a goal of trying to understand how he or she experiences the situation. Jot down what you believe is the other person's perspective on the matter.

____

____

____

Encouragement Opportunity 6

Practice accepting the roles, responsibilities, pressures, stresses and frustrations of other teammates. Identify other jobs on the team that you do not do and try to walk a mile in the shoes of your teammates. Instead of thinking how stressful or difficult your own job is, ask yourself, "What makes my teammates' jobs tough? What makes their jobs frustrating and stressful? What makes their jobs difficult?" Jot down some demanding responsibilities that others face.

____

____

____

____

____

Key Points on Sensitive-Listening Skills

1. Practice listening to other people's ideas without judging, but with a desire to understand.
2. Walk a mile in the shoes of your teammates to accept their unique problems from their worlds.
3. Hear things the first time they are said.

BEST TEAM SKILL #4—*EMPATHIC-RESPONDING SKILLS*

Empathic-responding skills are the skills of not only (1) sensing the other person's feelings but also (2) communicating those feelings back to him or her. (Sensitive-listening skills help you understand another person's perspective, whereas empathic-responding skills help you understand another person's feelings.)

Empathic-responding skills include:

1. Demonstrating an understanding of the facts about the other person's world (sensitive listening).
2. In consideration of those facts, sensing the other person's surface feelings.
3. Communicating surface feelings (e.g., anger).
4. Sensing possible deeper feelings (e.g., hurt).
5. Judging if it is appropriate to communicate sensing the other person's possible deeper feelings.
6. Communicating those deeper feelings, if appropriate.

Encouragement Opportunity 7—*Listening and sharing feelings*

Think about another person with whom you disagree on a matter. This time, instead of thinking about how he or she *thinks* about the issue, think about how this person *feels* about the situation. Use feeling words to describe this person's emotions. The next time you communicate with the person, communicate your understanding of his or her feelings. For example, "Bob, I sensed that you were really disappointed that I was late all last week and let the team down."

With whom can you use your empathic-responding skills to communicate that you understand the person's positive or negative feelings?

____

____

Encouragement Opportunity 8

How, in your opinion, is this other person feeling (not how he or she should feel according to you)?

____

____

____

____

____

How will you communicate your understanding of the person's feelings to him or her?

____

____

____

____

____

Key Points on Empathic-Responding Skills

1. Listen for the feelings underneath the person's words.
2. Communicate what you sense the person feels without adding what you think he or she *should* feel.

BEST TEAM SKILL #5—*QUESTIONING SKILLS*

Questioning skills are skills designed to help you gain relevant information from a person in a way that is safe, encouraging and non-threatening.

Questioning skills include:

1. Asking open-ended questions (questions that have more than a one-word answer or "yes" or "no" answer).
2. Asking questions to gather information rather than to judge the other person.
3. Asking questions using a safe tone and open body language.
4. Avoiding asking questions to which you already know the answer.
5. Asking questions to change the focus of the conversation when it is going in an unproductive direction.
6. Asking only one question at a time.
7. Avoiding jumping on any of the other person's answers, which results in making questions threatening.

Encouragement Opportunity 9—*Helping shy people to open up*

You have a teammate who is shy and only responds with "yes" or "no" answers when asked questions. You really want to help the person feel more comfortable with you. How could you use your questioning skills to help the shy person open up?

____

____

____

Key Points on Questioning Skills

1. Ask questions to gather more information to help your teammate.
2. Ask open-ended questions in a non-threatening way.

BEST TEAM SKILL #6—*PERSONALIZING SKILLS*

Personalizing skills are the skills of observing something unique and positive in other individuals.

Personalizing skills include:

1. Observing positive uniqueness in each individual.
2. Sharing unique qualities, talents, etc. to communicate recognition of their specialness.
3. Avoiding the tendency to dehumanize people by grouping them into categories (for example, by saying "you people" or referring to a person by his or her position on the team rather than as an individual). The fact is that you are like other people in many ways and they are different from each other in many ways. Each person is unique.
4. Personalizing is the ultimate way to humanize a person because it shows the person that you have taken time to understand him or her as a special, unique individual.

Encouragement Opportunity 10—*Personalizing each teammate*

Focus on each of your teammates and ask yourself this question: How is each person unique and special in a positive way?

____

____

____

____

____

____

Encouragement Opportunity 11

Share your personalizing observations with each teammate.

____

____

____

____

____

____

Key Points on Personalizing Skills

1. Make it a point to help every individual feel special and unique in a positive way.
2. Avoid the tendency to dehumanize people by grouping them into categories.

BEST TEAM SKILL #7—*ENTHUSIASM SKILLS*

Enthusiasm skills are verbal and non-verbal skills that communicate your excitement about the ideas, interests or potential of others. Enthusiasm adds energy to the person.

Enthusiasm skills include:

1. Listening for other people's claims-to-fame. Claims-to-fame are proud moments and achievements in a person's life. In each claim-to-fame is a number of assets, strengths and resources that can be used to motivate the person. (For example, "Ed, your team won the state championship [claim-to-fame]. That tells us you have both artistic and team talents. We could sure use those talents.")
2. Getting enthused about proud achievements from the teammate's last job.
3. Speaking enthusiastically about the interests of others.
4. Expressing yourself enthusiastically (facial gestures, wide-eyed) in response to other people's ideas.
5. Conditioning yourself to spot and respond to things that are important to others and let them know you heard them.
6. Basing your enthusiasm on what is important to others, not what is important to you. For example, if someone gets an old, beat-up car that is their first car, experience it as they do, not as you feel about their car.

Encouragement Opportunity 12—*Your enthusiasm energizes the team*

Think about some reasons for your team to get enthused. Talk up the positive things the team can be proud of. Identify five things about which the team can be enthused.

____

____

____

Encouragement Opportunity 13—*Getting enthused about individuals*

What are some of the things you can get enthused about with each of your teammates?

Share your enthusiasm with your teammates and watch their faces beam! Who has told you something recently to which you responded robotically, without enthusiastically experiencing their personal feelings?

Key Points on Enthusiasm Skills

1. Condition yourself to become enthused about other people's positive experiences.
2. Be quick to spot enthusiastic opportunities.

BEST TEAM SKILL #8—*AGREEMENT SKILLS*

Agreement skills are the skills to create an agreement trend between yourself and another teammate.

Agreement skills include:

1. Mirroring or using similar body movements, facial gestures, breathing patterns and tone of voice.
2. Asking questions in a way that is likely to produce a "yes" answer. (This is the use of agreement skills in combination with questioning skills.)
3. When disagreeing with what someone else has just said, starting with the word "and" instead of "but."

Encouragement Opportunity 14—*Creating an agreement trend*

Think of a person or persons with whom you disagree on some issue. List some areas where you agree.

____

____

____

In your next conversation, start by focusing on points of agreement before you begin to disagree in other areas.

Encouragement Opportunity 15

Practice getting in sync with people by using similar words, speaking at the same pace as they speak and using similar facial expressions and body gestures (mirroring).

Key Points on Agreement Skills

1. Whenever anyone speaks, quickly spot your areas of agreement.
2. Even when disagreeing, keep focused on getting into the agreement trend by using "and" instead of "but."

BEST TEAM SKILL #9—*MUTUALITY SKILLS*

Mutuality skills are the skills of finding common bonds, links or similarities between yourself and others. Mutuality skills are based upon the similarity-liking principle which suggests that the more I feel you are similar to me, the more I will tend to like you.

Mutuality skills include:

1. Listening closely to identify similarities between yourself and others.
2. Sharing your commonalties with the other person.
3. Using the word "we" or phrases similar to "people like us feel this way."

Encouragement Opportunity 16—*We are similar in many ways*

List at least three things you have in common with each of your teammates.

____

____

____

____

Share the similarities.

Encouragement Opportunity 17

Constantly talk about the things that unite or link the team together. What are some of the similarities and goals that link all of the teammates together?

____

____

____

____

____

____

Key Points on Mutuality Skills

1. Tune in to similarities whenever you meet someone.
2. Use the word "we" rather than "me" or "you."

BEST TEAM SKILL #10—*POSITIONING SKILLS*

Positioning skills are the skills that allow you to consciously plant yourself in a comfortable place in the mind of another person. You become real and solid rather than vague to that other person. Positioning allows the person to feel comfortable in relating to you because positioning anchors you in his or her mind.

Positioning skills include:

1. Sharing a little about your life, if the person asks.
2. Letting people know about your own interests.
3. Revealing some of your positive opinions.
4. Communicating where you are from and where you started.
5. Sharing your name so that everyone remembers it forever.
6. Being specific rather than vague. (For example, "I'm from up north" is vague, even elusive, whereas "I'm from Albany" is specific.)

Encouragement Opportunity 18—*Positioning yourself*

Think of those teammates who might not have you positioned in their minds. Make it a point to share a little more about yourself to make your image clearer in their minds. Jot down some ideas below.

____

____

____

____

____

Encouragement Opportunity 19—*Positioning others*

If another teammate isn't positioned in your mind, appears a little vague and leaves you somewhat uncomfortable, use your sensitive-listening, empathic-responding and questioning skills to learn more about that person. You are interested in the person's relationship with you as a teammate. Jot down some ideas below.

____

____

____

____

____

Key Points on Positioning Skills

1. People need to position you in order to feel comfortable with you as their teammate. Share a little of yourself rather than being vague, because vagueness makes it difficult to trust.
2. Positioning starts by making sure every teammate knows your name. Find some strategies to help people remember your name.

BEST TEAM SKILL #11—*ACCESSIBILITY SKILLS*

Accessibility skills are skills that communicate your availability when the team needs you.

Accessibility skills include:

1. Communicating where you can be reached if necessary.
2. Choosing to be involved in the team.
3. Keeping your door open to other teammates.
4. Attending staff or team meetings.
5. Being able to be counted on and being reliable.
6. Being available if needed.
7. Calling in when ill.
8. Calling in when you are going to be late.
9. Volunteering when it would help the team.
10. Resisting the tendency to "get sick" or make excuses when faced with responsibility.

Encouragement Opportunity 20—*Communicating your accessibility*

The next time the team needs someone to help on a specific project, go out of your way to make yourself accessible. Volunteer to contribute even though you could easily get out of it with an excuse.

Encouragement Opportunity 21

Join in with others. The team needs you. Instead of turning away from the team, make yourself more accessible. Involve yourself and encourage others to get involved with the team.

Key Points on Accessibility Skills

1. Make yourself, your skills and your services available to the team.
2. Be there when the team needs you. Be quick to volunteer.

BEST TEAM SKILL #12—*SENSORY-REPRESENTATIONAL SKILLS*

Sensory-representational skills help you understand another person's primary sensory-representation style (visual, auditory or tactile-kinesthetic) and then enable you to respond to that person in his or her most comfortable representational mode.

Sensory-representational skills include:

1. Listening for visual ("See you around"), auditory ("Can't wait to hear from you") or tactile-kinesthetic ("Keep in touch") references. The words a person uses tell you how he or she sees, hears or feels things.
2. Listening for speed of speech (visual is fast; auditory is slower, organized, correctly pronounced speech; and tactile-kinesthetic is very slow).
3. Observing breathing patterns (visual breathes high in the chest, auditory is medium and tactile-kinesthetic breathes very low).
4. Observing eye accessing cues (visual looks up to access memory or create a visual image, auditory looks at ear level and tactile-kinesthetic looks down to reflect or feel).
5. Decoding sensory-representational style.
6. Responding in a similar style ("I see what you mean," "I hear you" or "I have a feeling for what you are saying").

Encouragement Opportunity 22—*Accessing sensory-representational styles*

Identify the sensory styles of your teammates in order to better understand and communicate with each person. Using the above formula, determine if a person is visual, auditory or tactile.

____

____

____

____

Encouragement Opportunity 23—*Responding to a person based upon the person's sensory-representational style*

Practice speaking with people in their sensory styles. With visual people, use visual words ("Looks like you see it this way"). Speak faster and breathe more shallowly. With auditory people, use auditory words ("Sounds like you hear it this way"). Speak in a more controlled way, pronounce your words accurately and breathe more slowly. With tactile-kinesthetic people, use feeling words ("You seem to be feeling…"). Speak very slowly and with feeling.

Key Points on Sensory-Representational Skills

1. Constantly observe and assess other people's sensorial ways of representing life.
2. Condition yourself to speak to each person in his or her primary sensory-representational mode.

Principle 2
THE COOPERATION PRINCIPLE

"Competing Divides Us; Cooperating Multiplies Us"

Social-interest skills

Cooperative-listening skills

Credibility skills

Universalizing skills

Genuineness skills

Mutual-reliance skills

Conflict-resolution skills

COOPERATION SKILLS

USE OF THIS PARTICULAR SKILL	*INVITES THIS FEELING IN OTHERS*
13. Social-interest skills	"I feel a sense of belonging."
14. Cooperative-listening skills	"I feel like contributing."
15. Credibility skills	"I feel trusting."
16. Universalizing skills	"I feel linked with the team."
17. Genuineness skills	"I feel I can be real."
18. Mutual-reliance skills	"I feel supported and also supportive of the team."
19. Conflict-resolution skills	"I feel relief that our differences can be communicated and understood."

BEST TEAM SKILL #13—*SOCIAL-INTEREST SKILLS*

Social-interest skills are the skills you use to fulfill the needs of others to belong and to contribute to the team.

Social-interest skills include:

1. Communicating to each group member the ways in which he or she belongs or fits into the group. (For example, "As our team's receptionist, Betty, you put the clients in a positive frame of mind.")
2. Communicating to each other the ways in which each person contributes to the team. (For example, "Without our linemen up front, our backfield would be in deep trouble.")

Encouragement Opportunity 24—*Fulfilling each teammate's belonging needs*

List some teammates and identify how each makes the team a better team.

____

____

____

____

____

Share with your teammates how they belong.

Encouragement Opportunity 25—*Bringing in the out; bringing up the down*

If you sense that any teammates feel as if they are not a part of the team, be the sensitive one and show how the team considers them to be valued members.

Key Points on Social-Interest Skills

1. Help each teammate feel a part of things.
2. Be quick to remind each person how his or her contribution to the team makes a difference.

BEST TEAM SKILL #14—*COOPERATIVE-LISTENING SKILLS*

Cooperative-listening skills involve listening to others to determine ways to cooperate with them for the purpose of benefiting the team.

Cooperative-listening skills include:

1. Resisting the tendency to compete and compare. (Avoid saying, "Oh, that's nothing, I can do better than that!")
2. Listening with a desire to help others.
3. Listening for similarities.
4. Listening for differences.
5. Listening to others to sense ways you can cooperate to benefit them.
6. Listening to others to sense ways that they can cooperate to benefit you.
7. Listening to discover insights that might mutually benefit all team members.

Encouragement Opportunity 26—*Cooperative listening*

The next time you are listening to a teammate speak and feel the need to compete or outdo, resist the tendency. Instead, get into the cooperative-listening mode. Think, "How can I understand what he or she is saying in a way that can benefit the whole team?"

Key Points on Cooperative-Listening Skills

1. Listen in the spirit of cooperation.
2. Listen for ways to cooperate. Listen for ways that the speaker can cooperate to help you.

BEST TEAM SKILL #15—*CREDIBILITY SKILLS*

Credibility skills are the skills of doing what you said you would do and having it done by the time you said it would be done. Credibility is proving yourself trustworthy by being consistent. The credible person can be counted on to follow through with a job.

Credibility skills include:

1. Telling the team what you will do and when it will be done.
2. Having the task completed on time for the team.
3. Retaining credibility by honestly communicating a new plan if you have not completed the job on time.
4. Returning borrowed items.
5. Keeping promises and commitments.
6. Showing up on time.

Encouragement Opportunity 27—*Establishing credibility with others*

Think of some promises you made to the team or some responsibility you have taken on for the team. Consider these promises a great opportunity to earn credibility with the team. What are some things you need to follow through on in order to earn credibility with the team?

___

___

___

When will you achieve these things?

___

___

Encouragement Opportunity 28

Practice winning even more credibility by following through on small things. For example, when you tell someone, "I'll call you at ten o'clock on Tuesday," make a note to call at exactly ten o'clock on Tuesday.

Key Points on Credibility Skills

1. The credible person is trustworthy. The trustworthy person is consistent and does what they said they would do. Do what you say you will do and have it done by the time you said it would be done.
2. Keep your promises and commitments. You'll be a rare person. When you keep your commitments, you keep your credibility. You can easily borrow money on credibility.
3. If you borrow something, give it back.

BEST TEAM SKILL #16—*UNIVERSALIZING SKILLS*

Universalizing skills take individual concerns and achievements and reframe them in such a way that the team can universally feel a part of them. For example, saying "Have the others on the team experienced what Melissa has experienced with her clients?" is an example of universalizing. Or by saying, "Donna, our whole team is proud of your winning the competition. We're proud to be on the same team," Donna can universalize by responding, "Well, without the support of you guys, I wouldn't have had the skills and the courage to enter and win. This is not my victory. This is our team's victory."

Universalizing skills include:

1. Showing how one person's concerns relate to the concerns of the group.
2. Positioning yourself and others in the context of the group.
3. At team meetings, universalizing skills can help keep the whole team interested and involved.

Encouragement Opportunity 29—*Universalizing means that as teammates, we are all affected by what is happening to each of us.*

You receive a card from a client thanking you for the great experience she had with you and your team. How can you universalize the thanks?

____

____

____

____

____

Key Points on Universalizing Skills

1. Reframe experiences by constantly universalizing. Think "team, we, our, us."
2. When individual concerns are addressed, keep the group together and involved by universalizing the concerns in ways that are relative to everyone.

BEST TEAM SKILL #17—*GENUINENESS SKILLS*

The skill of genuineness involves being real.

Genuineness skills include:

1. Choosing to be honest rather than dishonest.
2. Expressing your feelings from an "I feel" rather than from a "you should" perspective. (For example, saying "I don't feel like I am a part of the team" rather than "You should make me feel like part of the team.")
3. Asking yourself, "Will sharing my ideas bring us closer as a team?"
4. Being genuine means being real about both positive as well as negative feelings.

Encouragement Opportunity 30—*Being real*

Do you have an idea about how to improve something the team does but have not shared the idea? Using genuineness skills, how can you share your idea with the group?

____

____

____

Encouragement Opportunity 31

Rewrite the following statement more effectively by using genuineness skills: "You guys are no good. You are always putting me down because I don't work as fast as you!"

____

____

____

Key Points on Genuineness Skills

1. Choose to be honest rather than dishonest.
2. State your real feelings in a way that will bring the team closer and in a non-threatening way. Start with "I feel..." rather than "You should..."
3. Be honest and open in telling the team the positive feelings you have.

BEST TEAM SKILL #18—*MUTUAL-RELIANCE SKILLS*

Mutual-reliance skills are the skills that communicate our interdependence or reliance on each other to do our part.

Mutual-reliance skills include:

1. Completing your responsibilities with the support of others.
2. Supporting others to complete their responsibilities.
3. Relying on each other in times of need.
4. Reaching the beautiful balance between independence ("I don't need you") and dependence ("I can't do anything without you").

Encouragement Opportunity 32—*Interdependence*

Do you lean toward being independent, dependent or interdependent? What could you do to move toward greater interdependence by using mutual-reliance skills?

____

____

____

____

Encouragement Opportunity 33

Could you use more support from the team? Using your genuineness skills, how could you communicate your need for more support?

____

____

____

____

Encouragement Opportunity 34

Could someone on the team use a little more support from you?

____

____

____

If so, what could you do to encourage your teammate?

____

____

____

____

Key Points on Mutual-Reliance Skills

1. Mutual reliance means we can depend on each other; we are interdependent.
2. Show the team that you are not only accessible, you are reliable!

BEST TEAM SKILL #19—*CONFLICT-RESOLUTION SKILLS*

Conflict-resolution skills are the skills used to rebuild team unity when dissynergy occurs.

Conflict-resolution skills include:

1. Taking the initiative to communicate interest in resolving the conflict.
2. Discussing all of the benefits of a unified team.
3. Expressing interest in learning more about the concerns or feelings of others.
4. Demonstrating how it would be mutually beneficial to resolve the conflict.
5. Reviewing sensitive-listening, empathic-responding and agreement skills.

Encouragement Opportunity 35—*Steps in resolving conflicts*

Use the following conflict-resolution process:

1. Party A shares his or her real thoughts and feelings about the conflict while Party B listens to understand Party A's view without judging.
2. Party B shares back Party A's thoughts and feelings until Party A is convinced that Party B understands (not necessarily agrees, but understands).
3. Party B shares his or her genuine thoughts and feelings while Party A listens to understand without judging.
4. Party A shares back Party B's thoughts and feelings until Party B feels understood.
5. Resolve the conflict by focusing on both parties' needs and proceed in the spirit that resolution is important for the team. The needs of both parties must be understood to benefit both sides.

Key Points on Conflict-Resolution Skills

1. Understand the facts and feelings of the other side before presenting your side.
2. State your side using genuineness skills ("I feel..." instead of "You should...").
3. Keep looking for agreement trends and mutuality.
4. Recognize that resolving the conflict benefits both parties and, as importantly, the entire team.

Phase II
EXPANDING THE MATRIX OF OUR MINDS

Focus on Thinking

Principle 3
THE FOCUS PRINCIPLE

"Determining Our Destination Determines Our Destiny"

Shared-vision skills

Mutual-determinism skills

Anticipation skills

Choosing skills

Self-starting skills

Goal-centering skills

FOCUS SKILLS

USE OF THIS PARTICULAR SKILL	*INVITES THESE TEAM THOUGHTS*
20. Shared-vision skills	"Our team has a common purpose."
21. Mutual-determinism skills	"It's up to us. We have all we need. We have the full commitment from each other."
22. Anticipation skills	"We are aware of the barriers on our road to success. We will develop a plan to solve the problems up front."
23. Choosing skills	"Because we are success-focused, we simply make the choices along the way that will lead us closer to our goal."
24. Self-starting skills	"It's up to each of us to take responsibility to keep ourselves going."
25. Goal-centering skills	"We are staying focused on the situation and on the solution that will lead to our goal, not to our own individual egos."

BEST TEAM SKILL #20—*SHARED-VISION SKILLS*

Shared-vision skills are the skills to identify, record and commit to mutual goals.

Shared-vision skills include:

1. Identifying a goal or series of goals that the team will achieve.
2. Listing measurable ways that make the team aware of the moment when that goal is achieved.
3. Recording the date or time when the goal will be achieved.
4. Mutually committing to achieving the goal.

Encouragement Opportunity 36—*Creating the goal, sharing the vision*

What goals will the team achieve?

____

____

____

____

Encouragement Opportunity 37—*Defining the time the goals will be achieved*

By what date will the goals be achieved?

____

____

____

____

Encouragement Opportunity 38

How will we know that the goals have been achieved?

____

____

____

____

Encouragement Opportunity 39—*Making the commitment*

Write down the names of the teammates who want to share the vision and make a commitment to achieve the team's goals by the stated dates.

____

____

____

____

Key Points on Shared-Vision Skills

1. The only people who ever reach their dreams are those who have them.
2. The team can only achieve the goals that it has. The goals are the reason for the existence of the team.
3. Make a commitment to share the vision together. The team needs everyone!

BEST TEAM SKILL #21—*MUTUAL-DETERMINISM SKILLS*

Mutual-determinism skills are the skills that take charge of the team's destiny.

Mutual-determinism skills include:

1. Recognizing that "It's up to us!"
2. Becoming a self-determined team rather than a luck-determined team.
3. Believing that the team's choices, rather than chance, affect the team's destiny.
4. Making choices that are consistent with moving closer to the goal (compassing).
5. Operating based on the conviction that the team has, or can acquire, all it needs to reach the goal.

Encouragement Opportunity 40—*Designing our own destiny*

Something dawned on your team today, the day of mutual-determinism. Your team is starting to realize that you actually have control over your future and your destiny. You can determine whether or not you reach your goals. You realize that putting a man on the moon or curing polio had to be harder than achieving your team's goals. Some "determined" team mutually agreed to those goals and achieved its dream. Is it possible that if your team uses mutual-determinism skills, you will realize that you, not luck, determine your future? The answer is yes. Your team's destiny is either determined by you or by other things.

Build a case to encourage the team to grow from helplessness to mutual-determinism. Make two points which prove that the team controls its destiny.

____

____

Key Points on Mutual-Determinism Skills

1. Our future is determined by either (a) us (mutual-determinism) or (b) not us (fate, luck, superstition or the stars). Let's become determined.
2. Believe we can or believe we can't. Either way, we will be determined to prove our point. So, let's believe we can!

BEST TEAM SKILL #22—*ANTICIPATION SKILLS*

Anticipation skills are the skills to see the barriers to the goals that lie ahead. After recognizing that we have control over our destiny with mutual-determinism skills, we look into the future, determined and motivated by our shared vision. We are becoming empowered to take the next step—spotting barriers that we may encounter. Through anticipation skills, we can detect and deal with these barriers.

Anticipation skills include:

1. Thinking into the future and preparing for obstacles (like equipment breaking down).
2. Anticipating the needs of other teammates.
3. Anticipating potential crisis points in the future.
4. Planning to avoid problems, crises, etc.

Encouragement Opportunity 41—*Anticipation*

Look ahead and anticipate every possible problem on the way to your shared vision.

____

____

____

____

____

____

Encouragement Opportunity 42

Find ways to prevent or solve every possible future problem up front by anticipation thinking.

____

____

____

____

____

____

Key Points on Anticipation Skills

1. The best teams think prevention.
2. Plan ahead. It will give your team the differential competitive edge.

BEST TEAM SKILL #23—*CHOOSING SKILLS*

Choosing skills involve making the most effective and efficient choices that will most directly lead to the team's goals.

Choosing skills include:

1. When facing a situation, asking yourself, "Which choice is the progress choice, and which is the regress choice?" The progress choice is the choice which will take you closer to your goal. The regress choice takes you farther away.
2. Choosing and acting upon the progress choice.

Encouragement Opportunity 43—*Choosing for success*

What are some choices the team needs to make? Which choice will lead the team closer to the shared vision (goal)? Make that choice. That's the progress choice.

____

____

____

____

____

Key Points on Choosing Skills

1. Your team's destiny is determined by its moment-to-moment choices.
2. If your team keeps making the progress choice, you will keep progressing.

BEST TEAM SKILL #24—*SELF-STARTING SKILLS*

Self-starting skills are the skills you use to motivate yourself into action.

Self-starting skills include:

1. Associating enormous pleasure with taking action.
2. Associating substantial pain with procrastinating.
3. Doing the unpleasant things first to get them off your mind.
4. Learning to like the things that you have to do.
5. Being your own source of inspiration.
6. Using positive self-talk to get moving.
7. Creating momentum for teammates.
8. Motivating yourself by visualizing achieving your goal.
9. Recognizing that each on-course action moves your team one step closer to its dream.
10. Constantly reminding yourself that "doing it is the best way to get it done."

Encouragement Opportunity 44—*Creating momentum*

Prove Newton's Law wrong. The law states that a body at rest tends to stay at rest until acted upon by an outside force. Prove that you can get yourself started without any outside force pushing you. Make a commitment to become a self-starter. Take pride in your ability to get started and keep going with motivational energy generated inside yourself. In which areas of your life do you need to become more self-starting?

____

____

____

Encouragement Opportunity 45

Associate massive amounts of negative feelings with the areas you want to develop as a self-starter. For example, if you tend to be late, make it painful to be late. See yourself as a burden to the team. Next, associate massive amounts of pleasure with being on time. This will result in gaining the respect and credibility of teammates, living up to the promises you made to the team to be on time and feeling good.

Negative associations:

____

____

____

Positive associations with self-starting:

____

____

____

Key Points on Self-Starting Skills

1. The momentum for your life must start with you.
2. Ultimately, no one but you can start you. Once you are started, no one but you can stop you.

BEST TEAM SKILL #25—*GOAL-CENTERING SKILLS*

Goal-centering skills are the skills to focus on the situation and the solution to a problem. This focus will lead to achieving the team's goal and will keep you from focusing on your own or the team's ego.

Goal-centering skills include:

1. Analyzing the situation rather than analyzing who is to blame.
2. Staying focused on the goal instead of looking good personally.
3. Refusing to relate one's worth with one's performance.
4. Recognizing the relationship between one's performance and team achievements.
5. Choosing to correct rather than to blame.
6. Seeing mistakes as opportunities to learn from the information gained.

Encouragement Opportunity 46—*Staying on the goal and off the blame*

Think of a recent time when the team missed a goal, faced a setback or failed at something. How much negative energy did the team devote to blaming or defending? How much positive, constructive energy was spent focusing on the situation and finding the best solution to reach the goal (goal-centering)?

Having acquired goal-centering skills, how could the team handle the same situation again?

____

____

____

____

____

Encouragement Opportunity 47

Two teammates fail in a situation. One teammate's reaction (ego-centered) is to conclude, "I failed because I am worthless, I'm no good and I'm stupid." The other teammate (goal-centered) observes, "The only reason I failed was because I didn't have all the information. If I want to do better, I'll have to ask more questions next time."

In what areas of your life could you be more goal-centered?

____

____

____

____

____

Key Points on Goal-Centering Skills

1. Make team goals more important than individual egos.
2. Keep focused on what counts. Focus on the situation and finding the best solution to reach the shared vision.
3. Become an architect of the future, not an archeologist digging up the past. Stay focused on what matters—the goal!

Principle 4
THE RESPECT PRINCIPLE

"Centering on Each Other's Strengths Builds Our Force"

Self-encouragement skills

Asset-focusing skills

Liability-into-asset skills

Relating-individual-assets-to-team-goal skills

Respecting skills

Expectation skills

RESPECT SKILLS

USE OF THIS PARTICULAR SKILL	*INVITES THESE TEAM THOUGHTS*
26. Self-encouragement skills	"Each of us will take personal responsibility to keep our own self in an encouraged state."
27. Asset-focusing skills	"Our team focus is on constantly reinforcing each other's assets, strengths and resources."
28. Liability-into-asset skills	"Individual qualities which at first glance might appear to be negative could actually be positive qualities in disguise that can be useful for the team. Let's look for ways we can each contribute by turning negatives into positives."
29. Relating-individual-assets-to-team-goal skills	"We know what our team goal is. We know the assets of each teammate. We need to constantly remind each other how vital these skills, assets and strengths are to the team's success."
30. Respecting skills	Communicating to each other our confidence and faith in simple words: "I believe in you. You can do it" or "We can do it."
31. Expectation skills	"We expect to succeed. We have no doubt that we will continue onward, no matter what, and we will reach our goal."

BEST TEAM SKILL #26—*SELF-ENCOURAGEMENT SKILLS*

Self-encouragement skills are the skills to bring out your own best.

Encouragement Opportunity 48—*Building yourself*

Identify and list your strengths, assets and hidden resources.

____

____

____

Encouragement Opportunity 49—*Your greatest achievement*

Recall your greatest achievement and identify the assets that it took to achieve that goal. Write them down.

____

____

____

Encouragement Opportunity 50—*Your physical resources*

What physical strengths do you possess that could help the team reach its goal?

____

____

____

Encouragement Opportunity 51—*Your social resources*

What social strengths do you possess that could help the team reach its goal?

____

____

____

Encouragement Opportunity 52—*Your technical resources*

What technical strengths do you possess that could help the team reach its goal?

____

____

____

Encouragement Opportunity 53—*Your educational resources*

What educational strengths do you possess that could help the team reach its goal?

____

____

____

Encouragement Opportunity 54—*Your intellectual resources*

What intellectual strengths do you possess that could help the team reach its goal?

____

____

____

Encouragement Opportunity 55—*Your creative resources*

What creative strengths do you possess that could help the team reach its goal?

____

____

____

Encouragement Opportunity 56—*Your personality resources*

What personality strengths do you possess that could help the team reach its goal?

____

____

____

Encouragement Opportunity 57—*Your spiritual resources*

What spiritual strengths do you possess that could help the team reach its goal?

____

____

____

Key Points on Self-Encouragement Skills

1. Put your best foot forward. The team needs you to be at your best. Stop dwelling on what's wrong with you; that doesn't work. Highlight what's right with you.
2. Consider all of your assets, strengths and resources. Focus on how you can best make a contribution to the team.

BEST TEAM SKILL #27—*ASSET-FOCUSING SKILLS*

Asset-focusing skills are skills that center on the strengths of others. They are similar to the self-encouragement skills you have just learned, but efforts are focused on your teammates.

Encouragement Opportunity 58—*Building your teammates*

Identify at least three strengths, assets and resources of each of your teammates. You can refer to the categories for self-encouragement skills, but don't be limited by those categories. Think of some qualities about each person that you enjoy or that make the team better.

____

____

____

____

____

Encouragement Opportunity 59—*Sharing your observations of your teammates' strengths*

Write your teammates' assets and strengths on a piece of paper. At the next team meeting, share them with each team member.

Key Points on Asset-Focusing Skills

1. We can't pick people up by putting them down. The only way we can lift people up is by elevating their assets and strengths.
2. Make it a point to constantly see what is right in people and immediately share it with others.
3. Remember, the better our teammates do, the better our team does, and the better each one of us does. We want to build each other.

BEST TEAM SKILL #28—*LIABILITY-INTO-ASSET SKILLS*

Liability-into-asset skills involve spotting the positive counterpart to what seems to be a negative aspect of a teammate.

Liability-into-asset skills include:

1. Identifying what seems to be a liability (e.g., stubbornness).
2. Creatively sensing whether that trait can actually have a positive element that could benefit the team (e.g., stubbornness can also be determination and the team needs this person's determination).

Encouragement Opportunity 60—*Liability-into-asset switching*

At first glance, the following traits appear to be negative. However, if you use liability-into-asset skills, you will be able to see the buried resources.

LIABILITY	*ASSET*
Nitpicker	____________________
Too serious	____________________
Overly adventurous	____________________
Follows the beat of a different drummer	____________________
Bossy	____________________
Clowns around	____________________

Encouragement Opportunity 61—*Using liability-into-asset skills on yourself*

What traits do you possess that you think are negative and are liabilities to your personality?

____

____

____

Using liability-into-asset skills, can you see a positive asset in any of your "liabilities"?

____

____

____

Key Points on Liability-into-Asset Skills

1. Be slow to judge a person's negative points. They could be assets in disguise. The team needs the person who follows the beat of a different drummer for creative thinking and daring innovation. The team needs the stubborn person to follow through. The team needs the nitpicker to anticipate problems and iron out the details.
2. What you might have thought was wrong with you may actually be the reason you overcame challenges in the past. Through liability-into-assets skills, you might be surprised to learn that underneath the liability was an asset.

BEST TEAM SKILL #29—*RELATING-INDIVIDUAL-ASSETS-TO-TEAM-GOAL SKILLS*

Relating-individual-assets-to-team-goal skills are the skills of (1) identifying an individual's assets, strengths and resources; (2) turning a person's liabilities into assets; and (3) making the connection between what the teammate has and what the team needs.

Encouragement Opportunity 62—*Individual-assets-to-team-goals*

1. Identify individual assets, strengths and resources by referring to what you listed in asset-focusing skills (Skill #27).
2. List any liabilities that can be turned into assets.
3. Visualize team goals.
4. Creatively identify ways that each person's strengths are needed by the team.
5. At the next team meeting, point out to each person the need for his or her unique strengths to help the team reach its goal.

Encouragement Opportunity 63

How can your own assets, strengths and resources contribute to reaching the shared vision or the goals of the team?

____

____

____

____

____

____

Key Points on Relating-Individual-Assets-to-Team-Goal Skills

1. Constantly sense what the team needs. Survey the team and ask yourself, "Who has the assets and resources that the team needs?"
2. Share with the individual your observations that the team could use his or her assets, strengths and resources.

BEST TEAM SKILL #30—*RESPECTING SKILLS*

Respecting skills are skills that communicate among teammates their confidence in each other.

Respecting skills include:

1. Trusting each teammate to handle his or her responsibilities and resisting the tendency to rescue.
2. Communicating "I believe in you. You have many assets and strengths. You are the kind of person who gets things done."
3. Reminding each person of his or her assets and strengths.
4. Treating each person like he or she has the qualities necessary to get the job done.

Encouragement Opportunity 64—*Respecting Others*

Respecting means communicating "I believe in you." How could you communicate respect to each of your teammates who is currently facing a challenge without solving the problem? Start with each person's assets, strengths and resources. Add his or her liabilities turned into assets. Keep encouraging the person by conveying, "You can do it!"

Who in particular could use your respect? Using your respecting skills, what will you do to encourage this person?

____

____

____

____

Encouragement Opportunity 65—*Respecting yourself*

Self-respect, like respecting another, is communicating to yourself, "Hang in there. You can do it. You have many assets, strengths and resources to achieve this goal." Put yourself in a highly resourceful, empowered, self-encouraging state and do it!

Take a few seconds and talk to yourself. Prove that through self-encouragement and respecting skills, you can motivate yourself into action.

Key Points on Respecting Skills

1. Treat teammates as though they already have the qualities that the team needs them to develop.
2. Be slow to rescue. Rescuing is a subtle clue that says, "We have lost faith in you." Instead, point out the person's assets, strengths and resources, as well as the team's belief in the person. Stay close with your encouragement.
3. Constantly develop your own self-respect. Believe in yourself and your ability to do things today that you could not do yesterday.

BEST TEAM SKILL #31—*EXPECTATION SKILLS*

Expectation skills are the skills that communicate high expectations for the team.

Expectation skills include:

1. Communicating "Considering all of our assets together, we can do it!"
2. Encouraging raising our standards.
3. Proceeding with certainty and combating doubts.

Encouragement Opportunity 66—*What you expect is what you get*

Consider all the skills the team developed by understanding the *respect principle,* and list five powerful reasons to tell your team why you expect them to succeed—to reach the shared vision. Take your time and record your five reasons. Then, make sure you communicate these reasons to your team at a team meeting.

1. ______________________________

____

____

2. ______________________________

____

____

3. ______________________________

____

____

4. ____

____

____

5. ____

____

____

Key Points on Expectation Skills

1. More often than not, you get what you expect.
2. Expect big. Raise your standards. Your motivation will rise with your raised standards.

Principle 5
THE REALITY PRINCIPLE

"Accepting 'What Is' Is Our Only Real Starting Point"

Objectivity skills

Acceptance skills

Humor skills

Relabeling skills

Rational-thinking skills

Assertiveness skills

Welcoming-criticism skills

REALITY SKILLS

USE OF THIS PARTICULAR SKILL	*INVITES THESE TEAM THOUGHTS*
32. Objectivity skills	"Here is where we are. These are the facts we face."
33. Acceptance skills	"We can't change that fact. And it may not be worth our energy to change other facts. So let's move on and focus on what we can and will change."
34. Humor skills	"We had five setbacks in a row. The universe is zeroing in on our team, trying to hold us back. We must be important."
35. Relabeling skills	"It's not a tragedy. It's a minor inconvenience."
36. Rational-thinking skills	"It's not what happens to all of us on the team that affects us. What affects us is the way we think about what happened."
37. Assertiveness skills	"Everyone on the team has the right to offer his or her opinion if it is intended to improve the team."
38. Welcoming-criticism skills	"We can grow from any information, whether positive or negative, as long as it is useful."

BEST TEAM SKILL #32—*OBJECTIVITY SKILLS*

Objectivity skills are the skills used to perceive reality clearly, undiluted by your own personal needs, wishes or "shoulds."

Objectivity skills include:

1. Recognizing that reality is what it is. It is not what we wish it to be in our minds.
2. Recognizing that reality is what it is. It is not what we think it should be in our minds.
3. Recognizing that the friendliest place to start on the road to the team's goal is with reality. Over the long run, the facts are always friendlier than wishes and "shoulds."

Encouragement Opportunity 67—*Developing objectivity*

Being objective means having the skills to see what really is without interference from our own wishes and shoulds. Being objective saves us a lot of frustration down the road, because we are living on false beliefs when we are not being objective. So today is a long-term opportunity for the team. What are some areas where we need to develop our objectivity skills to see things as they really are?

____

____

____

____

____

Encouragement Opportunity 68—*Objectivity as a motivator*

Being objective and facing reality indicate that we are quite a rare team. We have gone beyond most teams that try to fool themselves or "should" on themselves by twisting reality to fit their own needs or wants. This indicates our own inner security and the team's willingness to face and accept what is and adjust its plans to the shared vision. Describe a time when the team proved that facing the facts is the friendliest place to start.

____

____

____

____

____

Key Points on Objectivity Skills

1. The facts are the facts. On the road to our shared dream, we will start with what is. That is the only real way we can securely move to what will be.
2. Every time one of our teammates strays from reality and objectivity and uses the word "wish" or "should," by the end of the sentence that person is going to be frustrated. Help the person by asking, "What's your plan to improve the situation?"

BEST TEAM SKILL #33—*ACCEPTANCE SKILLS*

Acceptance skills are the skills to face and immediately accept the things that the team chooses not to change.

Acceptance skills include:

1. When facing a major barrier, asking two questions: (1) Can we change the situation? and (2) Is it worth our energy to change the situation?
2. When deciding that the situation would not be worth changing or can't be changed, then accepting it.
3. Sweet surrendering (recognizing that "what is, is").
4. Swiftly moving to change situations that can be changed.
5. Optimistically recognizing that by accepting the things the team chooses not to change, its energies are more focused on positive, realistic goals.

Encouragement Opportunity 69—*Acceptance*

What situation is currently frustrating the team?

____

____

____

____

As a team, ask yourselves if your team could overcome this barrier using your creative minds. Would it be worth the team's energies to overcome the obstacle?

____

____

____

Encouragement Opportunity 70

If the team concludes that (1) it can't overcome the barrier or (2) the team's energies could be better spent in other directions, use your acceptance skills and move on. If the team concludes that it would be (1) possible and (2) worth it for the team to use its energies to rise above the barrier, then the team can use perceptual-alternative skills. Will the team change or accept the situation?

____

____

____

Encouragement Opportunity 71

When accepting what (1) can't be changed or (2) won't be changed, the team agrees that it will not bring up the topic again, unless conditions change. The team agrees that it will not frustrate itself by "wishing" or "shoulding." Acceptance means accepting that "what is, is!"

____

____

____

Encouragement Opportunity 72

In what situation does the team need to use more acceptance skills?

____

____

____

Key Points on Acceptance Skills

1. What is, is!
2. If we cannot change something or we don't want to use our energies to change it, then we sweet surrender to it. We accept it. The issue is dropped. Our focus is on a bigger issue!

BEST TEAM SKILL #34—*HUMOR SKILLS*

Humor skills are the skills to face inconvenient realities by humbly admitting that events in the universe may not be organized around our team personally.

Humor skills include:

1. Gaining perspective by recognizing that each of us is one of six billion people on earth. It is unlikely that anyone is so important that red lights or traffic jams are arranged around him or her personally.
2. When facing what appears to be a setback, instead of getting uptight, humorously asking, "Why is the universe treating me like this today? Doesn't it know who I am?"

Encouragement Opportunity 73—*Getting perspective*

The next time you are caught in an inconvenience like getting in a slow line at the bank or supermarket, where all the other lines are moving faster, humorously ask the people in front of you if they met earlier and agreed to frustrate you.

Encouragement Opportunity 74

Find the longest traffic light you know—the one you always just miss. Time it. You will start to find patterns that are fairly consistent, like green for one minute, red for one minute and a yellow signal. Now, facing your reality, humorously ask yourself if this pattern shifts with your presence!

Encouragement Opportunity 75

In a difficult situation that the universe has created for the team, humorously ask your teammates, "What is the worst that could possibly happen?" Even if the worst possible outcome did happen, is it possible that the team would still have options? If so, what would those options be?

The fact is that the team, under the worst of all circumstances, could still make it. Now, getting back to reality, if we can handle that, we can handle anything!

Encouragement Opportunity 76

Where could the team use a little more humor?

____

____

____

____

____

Key Points on Humor Skills

1. Life is too important to take seriously. Lighten up, because the team has things to accomplish.
2. The universe is not zeroing in on us personally. It rains because of atmospheric conditions, not because of us.
3. We could handle even worse than this and still make it!

BEST TEAM SKILL #35—*RELABELING SKILLS*

Relabeling skills are the skills to diminish the power of a potentially frustrating or volatile situation by looking at the experience in a different way and using less explosive, inflammatory and volcanic words to describe it.

Relabeling skills include:

1. Recognizing that events become what we label them.
2. Relabeling setbacks as mere annoyances.
3. If a project fails, remembering that there is a better way and the team has learned from the experience. Relabeling the experience as a learning opportunity enables us to grow. Labeling the experience as failing creates failure.
4. Recognizing that the most anything in life can be is a minor inconvenience rather than a tragedy or catastrophe.
5. Using the following words to describe a difficult situation: inconvenience, annoyance, disturbance, nuisance, hindrance. Relabeling skills diffuse a potentially volatile situation because events become what a person labels them.

Encouragement Opportunity 77—*Relabeling negatives (downgrading)*

Relabel your teammates' reactions to realistic experiences to take the sting out and give the team the motivation to keep on going.

TEAMMATE SAYS	*YOU RELABEL*
"I failed."	"________________________"
"I was rejected."	"________________________"
"It was terrible, awful."	"It was __________________"
"We are done, devastated."	"We are lucky because ______ ________________________"

Encouragement Opportunity 78—*Relabeling positives (upgrading)*

TEAMMATE SAYS	*YOU RELABEL*
"It was okay, I guess."	"It was awesome!"
"I'm doing alright."	"I'm turbo charged!"
"Our team will get by, maybe."	"________________________" (Hint: recall certainty skills)

Key Points on Relabeling Skills

1. Events become whatever we label them. Practice relabeling events in a way that motivates your team. Refuse to get caught up in downers.
2. Talk things up! Add life to routine by using relabeling skills.
3. Remember, the most anything can be is a simple inconvenience!

BEST TEAM SKILL #36—*RATIONAL-THINKING SKILLS*

Rational-thinking skills are skills to prove to our teammates that it's not what happens to us in life that affects us; rather, it's the way we look at things that affects us. Only we can choose how we look at things.

Rational-thinking skills include:

1. Using the A-B-C formula to deal rationally with a stressful situation, where
   - A is some *Activating* event, or something that happens to us.
   - B is our *Belief* about the situation that happens to us.
   - C is our *Consequent* emotion, or how we feel about the event.
2. Proving to the team that A does not cause C.
   - If A caused C, then everyone would have the same consequent emotion or feeling.
   - Because there are a number of different reactions or feelings to the same event (A), it proves that what actually caused C was B, the person's belief about the situation.
   - And the great news is that while we don't always control the situations we face in life, we do control B.

Encouragement Opportunity 79—*Rational-thinking*

Consider a current difficult situation the team is experiencing. Call the situation A. The situation is the activating event. The situation does not cause C, how the team feels (consequent emotion). What causes how the team feels is B, the team's beliefs about A or what the teammates tell themselves. If the team uses objectivity, acceptance, relabeling and human skills at B, the team will experience more positive emotions at C.

Now identify a few ways to look at the difficult situation by using rational-thinking skills.

A. Identify the situation.

____

____

____

B. Identify the team's beliefs about the situation.

____

____

____

C . How do you feel when you look at the same situation in a more rational way?

____

____

____

Key Points on Rational-Thinking Skills

1. What we think is what we feel.
2. It's not what happens to us in life that affects us. It's the way we look at what happens to us in life that affects us.

BEST TEAM SKILL #37—*ASSERTIVENESS SKILLS*

Assertiveness skills help you to state your feelings, thoughts and needs for the purpose of improving your relationship with the team in a way that will be effective.

Assertiveness skills include:

1. Being able to identify the differences between timidity, aggressiveness and assertiveness.

TIMID	*ASSERTIVE*	*AGGRESSIVE*
"Die and let live"	"Live and let live"	"Live and let die"
Avoiding expression of personal needs	Sharing needs to improve relationship with team	Domineering, wants to hurt or vent anger
Hurts self	Balanced	Hurts team

2. Assertiveness is designed to educate, inform and to build teammates as opposed to putting them down.
3. Assertiveness involves avoiding talking about a teammate behind his or her back. When assertiveness is occurring, it should be done with the motive of helping the other person to understand how you feel.
4. Assertiveness is not communicating, "I am right. You are wrong" (aggressiveness). Assertiveness is communicating, "I feel this way. I recognize you could feel differently. I believe that if you looked at the situation this way, it would be advantageous for the whole team."

ENCOURAGEMENT OPPORTUNITY 80—*Assertiveness*

Asserting oneself is most effectively accomplished by following these steps:

1. Pointing out something positive in the teammate.
2. Addressing the most important area that you feel needs development.

3. Discussing why it is a team problem, along with the desirable action or attitude.
4. Sensitively listening to the person's reaction.
5. Recommending a solution.
6. Noticing positive change.

Encouragement Opportunity 81

Where can you use some assertiveness skills?

____

____

____

____

____

Key Points on Assertiveness Skills

1. Take responsibility for sharing your concerns with the team in a personal way. Say "I feel" instead of "You should."
2. Assert yourself only if your motive is to help others become more aware of your needs in order to improve your relationship.

BEST TEAM SKILL #38—*WELCOMING-CRITICISM SKILLS*

Welcoming-criticism skills are the skills to listen to criticism in an open way in order to find opportunities to grow from the observations and assertions of others.

Welcoming-criticism skills include:

1. Listening to hear the whole story before immediately responding to any one part of the criticism.
2. Conveying open body language when being criticized.
3. Staying calm and breathing deeply.
4. Reassuring yourself that things will be okay and that you might actually learn something from the criticism which will help you grow.
5. Summarizing what the critic said and deciding objectively what information you can use to grow—and then using it.
6. Thanking the critic.

Encouragement Opportunity 82—*Handling criticism*

What could you have done differently in the past if you had used welcoming-criticism skills?

____

____

____

____

____

Encouragement Opportunity 83

Think of the last few times someone criticized you. Ask yourself whether there was a seed of truth in the criticism that could help you. If so, did you use it or fight it? Even less effectively, did you switch the topic and attack the critic? Refocus and ask yourself what you have learned from your past criticisms.

____

____

____

____

____

Key Points on Welcoming-Criticism Skills

1. Remember, criticism can be synonymous with a four-letter word—GROW.
2. Welcome criticism. Criticism provides information that winners use but losers fight.

Principle 6
THE OPTIMISM PRINCIPLE

"Believing Problems Have Solutions Gives Us the Advantage"

Overcoming-discouraging-belief skills

Certainty skills

Find-a-way skills

Perceptual-alternative skills

Optimistic-explanatory skills

OPTIMISM SKILLS

USE OF THIS PARTICULAR SKILL	*INVITES THESE TEAM THOUGHTS*
39. Overcoming-discouraging-belief skills	"Let's rise above our limited thinking. Let's think big. Let's think with courage!"
40. Certainty skills	"No problem. We can deal with whatever comes our way. Certainty gives us the competitive edge."
41. Find-a-way skills	"Let's not limit our vision of our future by the narrow, limited experiences of our past. Let's proceed as if every problem has a solution and use our unlimited, creative minds to find a way!"
42. Perceptual-alternative skills	"Let's look at this situation in an entirely new way."
43. Optimistic-explanatory skills	"This setback is related to the unique situation which occurred during this incident and does not affect our future actions."

BEST TEAM SKILL #39—*OVERCOMING-DISCOURAGING-BELIEF SKILLS*

Overcoming-discouraging-belief skills involve seeing through limited, discouraging beliefs that hold the team back. They also involve developing more optimistic and courageous beliefs to move the team forward.

Overcoming-discouraging-belief skills include:

1. Rising above thinking that the problem you face is impossible to overcome and concluding that, "Just because something seems impossible doesn't mean it can't be done." Impossible just means the world needs someone to find a way. Remind the team that at one time, running the four-minute mile seemed impossible, as did every other great achievement.
2. Rising above thinking that you shouldn't do anything that you can't do perfectly to thinking that you can learn from every action you take. Learning is more important than being perfect.
3. Rising above thinking that you're too small, too young, too old, too poor or too tired to thinking, "We have lots of assets, strengths and resources and we believe in ourselves."
4. Rising above thinking, "Until something outside of us changes, like the economy, the world or the competition, things are hopeless" to thinking, "We are the cause; we create the effects. When we change, the world outside of us changes. We can make things happen."
5. Translating discouraging beliefs into more rational optimistic and courageous beliefs.

DISCOURAGING BELIEFS	*COURAGEOUS BELIEFS BELIEFS*
"We must be perfect."	"We would like to be perfect. We want to be perfect, but we don't need to be perfect in order to move ahead."

DISCOURAGING BELIEFS	*COURAGEOUS BELIEFS BELIEFS*
"Things must go our way, or it would be terrible."	"Things are going to go the way they are going to go. We would prefer that things go the way we want them to, but we don't need things to go our way in order for us to keep on track."

Encouragement Opportunity 84—*Identifying discouraging beliefs*

What are some discouraging beliefs (fears, uncertainties, etc.) team members have that are keeping them from moving forward?

___

___

___

Encouragement Opportunity 85—*Develop more courageous beliefs*

What are some optimistic beliefs that you can help the team acquire in order to move forward?

___

___

___

Key Points on Overcoming-Discouraging-Belief Skills

1. Believe you can or believe you cannot. Either way, you will be right.
2. Impossible doesn't mean it cannot be done. It just means that the world is waiting for someone to do it.

BEST TEAM SKILL #40—*CERTAINTY SKILLS*

Certainty skills are the skills of proceeding confidently with the certainty of success.

Certainty skills include:

1. Constantly communicating to each other, "We can do it!"
2. Minimizing problems and maximizing total team potential. (For example, "That's no problem. We can handle something as small as that.")
3. Plowing forward. Keep on keeping on even when the team is down by ten runs in the bottom of the ninth inning. The person with certainty skills is sure the team will pull it off.
4. Giving our team the advantage by putting us in our most "resource-full" state, making our team more fully functioning. With all of our strengths at peak performance, we dramatically enhance our chance for victory.
5. Communicating, "Even though we don't know every challenge we are about to encounter in our future, we do know that we have the resources to handle them. We are certain we can."

Encouragement Opportunity 86—*Using certainty skills to proceed*

What challenge does your team face today or in the near future? How will you use your certainty skills to inspire your team into its most "resource-full" state and move the team forward?

____

____

____

____

Encouragement Opportunity 87

When are the most appropriate times to use certainty skills?

____

____

____

____

Key Points on Certainty Skills

1. Act as if you have what it takes, and don't doubt it for one second. Proceed with certainty against the challenges of the day.
2. Keep reminding yourself, "We aren't certain what challenges today holds for us. But we are certain we have the resources on our team to handle whatever we may face."

BEST TEAM SKILL #41—*FIND-A-WAY SKILLS*

Find-a-way skills are the skills to mobilize and use the unlimited inventory of ideas in the creative minds of the team members to find a way over the barriers on the way to the team's goals. "Find-a-wayers" have the ultimate advantage because they are charged up with the conviction that every problem has a solution.

Find-a-way skills include:

1. Believing that somewhere in the universe of the team's collective mind there is an answer to this problem.
2. Reminding the team of past times when they found a way.
3. Encouraging creative thinking. Let your mind explore new ideas without rejecting them until they have been thought through.
4. Encouraging all ideas, no matter how crazy they may seem.
5. Operating based on the idea that partial solutions are important contributions to total solutions.

Encouragement Opportunity 88—*Finding a way*

Revisit your team's goals from the *focus principle.* At your next team meeting, ask everyone to open up their mind by proceeding as if the way to achieve these goals were somewhere in the vastness of their creative mind. Proceed as if the answer will come together in pieces, like a puzzle. Again, no idea is stupid. Let the ideas flow. Record each idea. Watch what happens. Your team will find a way!

Key Points on Find-a-Way Skills

1. Never make the mistake of limiting the vision of your future by the narrow limited experience of your past.
2. In the vast realm of the alive, creative human mind, there are no limitations.
3. Proceed as if every problem has a solution.

BEST TEAMS SKILL #42—*PERCEPTUAL-ALTERNATIVE SKILLS*

Perceptual-alternative skills are the skills of perceiving the same old situation in many novel, creative ways.

E

What do you see? An "E"? Are there other alternate ways of perceiving this form? Could it be a "W" if turned sideways? How about an "M"? Could it be a ladder or part of a fork? What else could it be? Jot down the many different things you see in this form. No answer is wrong. Develop as many perceptual alternatives as you like.

Encouragement Opportunity 89

Focus in on a controversial issue for which you have a position that is uncompromising. You know exactly how you feel about this matter. You will soon take a tough test to determine if you are able to use perceptual-alternative skills. See if you can walk a mile in the shoes of someone who believes the exact opposite of you on this controversial issue. Present the other side of the story to the point that it is almost convincing to you.

____

____

____

____

____

Encouragement Opportunity 90

Identify some concerns, problems or frustrations the team is currently experiencing. Using perceptual-alternative skills, generate different ways of looking at or perceiving the situation, as you did when you looked at the "E" above.

PROBLEM	*PERCEPTUAL ALTERNATIVES*

Key Points on Perceptual-Alternative Skills

1. There are as many ways of looking at a situation as there are people. Perceptual-alternative skills are the skills used in generating numerous ways of looking at the same old situation.
2. When stuck on a problem, back off and create some perceptual alternatives. You'll see things differently immediately.

BEST TEAM SKILL #43—*OPTIMISTIC-EXPLANATORY SKILLS*

Optimistic-explanatory skills are the skills to explain setbacks in life as optimists do, as opposed to how pessimists do.

Optimistic-explanatory skills include:

1. Explaining setbacks as related to the situation as opposed to personal inadequacy. (Optimist: "It was a bad day." Pessimist: "I really blew it.")
2. Explaining setbacks as related to a temporary fact as opposed to a permanent condition. (Optimist: "I failed the math test yesterday." Pessimist: "I'm no good at spelling. I must be stupid.")
3. Explaining setbacks as related only to the subject at hand as opposed to all areas of life. (Optimist: "The first client didn't buy my product today. That affects nothing else in my life." Pessimist: "The first customer didn't buy anything. I am no good at selling. I am also no good and never will be good at anything.")

PESSIMISTIC EXPLANATION FOLLOWING REJECTION	*OPTIMISTIC EXPLANATION FOLLOWING REJECTION*
Personal: "I messed up."	Situation: "It was the setting."
Permanent: "I'll never be able to succeed at this."	Temporary: "It was just that time. That time is over."
Pervasive: "I'm not good at anything."	Specific: "This doesn't affect anything else in my life."

Encouragement Opportunity 91—*Using an optimistic-explanatory style*

You offer an idea to the team and it is overwhelmingly rejected. Some teammates even laugh at it. You feel upset and tell yourself that you are never going to suggest anything ever again.

How could you use an optimistic-explanatory style to get beyond your down thoughts (reread above)?

____

____

____

____

____

Key Points on Optimistic-Explanatory Skills

1. When facing an inconvenience, focus on the situation, not on yourself.
2. Remember, setbacks are temporary, not permanent.
3. Setbacks don't affect your whole life, just the situation.

Phase III
ACTION AND PROGRESS

Focus on Doing

Principle 7
THE PROGRESS PRINCIPLE

"Encouraging Progress Precedes Praising Success"

Becoming skills

Effort-focusing skills

Spotting-improvement skills

Contribution-recognition skills

Evaluating-action skills

Credit-sharing skills

Celebration skills

PROGRESS SKILLS

USE OF THIS PARTICULAR SKILL	*INVITES THESE TEAM ACTIONS*
44. Becoming skills	Team experiences itself in the process of becoming successful
45. Effort-focusing skills	Team notices individual efforts
46. Spotting-improvement skills	Team acts with the goal of improvement
47. Contribution-recognition skills	Team acts by recognizing each person's contribution
48. Evaluating-action skills	Team acts quickly to assess action
49. Credit-sharing skills	Teammates actively give credit, rather than taking it
50. Celebration skills	Teammates actively celebrate success together, including everyone

BEST TEAM SKILL #44—*BECOMING SKILLS*

Becoming skills are the skills of focusing on your team not as you are at the moment, but rather as you are in the process of becoming.

Becoming skills include:

1. Feeling your team in active motion, growing in the process of becoming your dream.
2. Choosing to constantly expand out of the comfort zone and stay in the process of becoming more and more each moment.
3. Focusing on your team as a process rather than a finished product.

Encouragement Opportunity 92—*Feeling yourself becoming*

Who are you in the process of becoming? Identify who you are in the process of becoming physically, socially, professionally, financially and spiritually.

Physically ____

____

____

Socially ____

____

____

Professionally ____

____

____

Financially ____

____

____

Spiritually ____

____

____

The moment you identify each personal goal, it is already happening because you are in process. The new you is taking shape.

Encouragement Opportunity 93—*What is your team in the process of becoming?*

See your team in process. Identify some areas in which your team is developing and is in the process of becoming.

____

____

____

____

____

Key Points on Becoming Skills

1. You are not a human being. You are a *human becoming.*
2. Your team is in the process of becoming more tomorrow than it is today, because of the actions you are taking today.

BEST TEAM SKILL #45—*EFFORT-FOCUSING SKILLS*

Effort-focusing skills are the skills to recognize the efforts made by yourself and others.

Effort-focusing skills include:

1. Emphasizing to yourself and others that focusing on effort is a more effective encourager than focusing on success or failure. When we focus on effort, people will make the effort. When people make the effort, they will progress. But if we focus only on success or failure, people will become discouraged. Then they will only make an effort in those instances in which they believe ahead of time they will succeed.
2. Sensitizing yourself to notice efforts.
3. Encouraging people to make the effort in order to gain knowledge and experience which will be useful to them in the future.
4. Supporting a person who has made an effort and is discouraged because they feel like they failed. Use your effort-focusing skills to help people feel good about their efforts.
5. Remembering that efforts are all we have. When people are discouraged, they are no longer making an effort, and without effort, there is no growth.
6. Speaking the language of effort focusing. (For example, "It looks like you really worked hard on that" or "You spent a lot of time thinking that through, and it sure shows" or "You have persistence, and it's going to pay off.")

Encouragement Opportunity 94—*Effort-focusing*

One of your teammates falls short of her goal even though she worked tirelessly to try to achieve it. She is discouraged. How could you encourage her even though she didn't reach her goal and is feeling like she really let the team down? What could you say to her?

Encouragement Opportunity 95—*Effort-focusing on a teammate*

With whom can you use effort-focusing skills today?

How will you use effort-focusing with this person?

Encouragement Opportunity 96—*Effort-focusing on the team*

Could your team use some effort-focusing?

How will you use effort-focusing to motivate continued action?

____

____

____

Key Points on Effort-Focusing Skills

1. Recognize effort over success, because no effort means no success.
2. Spot every little extra effort people make. It will increase their efforts.

BEST TEAM SKILL #46—*SPOTTING-IMPROVEMENT SKILLS*

Spotting-improvement skills are the skills in noticing any improvements a teammate is making.

Spotting-improvement skills include:

1. Sensitizing yourself to spot any improvements in yourself and others.
2. Doing a before-and-after comparison on yourself and others. Tell other people how much they have improved over a time in their past by saying, "Remember when you struggled to do this? Now you are comfortable doing twice as much. That's improvement."
3. Speaking the language of improvement spotting. (For example, "Look at the progress you are making" or "You're improving in..." or "You may not feel you have reached your goal yet, but look how far you have come.")

Encouragement Opportunity 97—*Spotting improvement in a teammate*

Which teammate has shown a great deal of improvement lately? As you reread the three points above, what will you tell this person to really encourage him or her by using spotting-improvement skills?

____

____

____

Encouragement Opportunity 98—*Spotting team improvement*

Think about where your team was at some point in the past. Think of how the team has improved. Write down some specific areas where the team has improved, and share what you have written with the team.

____

____

____

Encouragement Opportunity 99—*Spotting your own improvement*

Where have you shown improvement on the job?

____

____

____

What can you do today that you couldn't do when you started?

____

____

____

Key Points on Spotting-Improvement Skills

1. Notice every bit of improvement in yourself and others. Tell other people how they have improved!
2. Think improvement every day.

BEST TEAM SKILL #47—*CONTRIBUTION-RECOGNITION SKILLS*

Contribution-recognition skills are the skills in pointing out to others how their efforts contribute to the progress of the team.

Contribution-recognition skills include:

1. Talking up a person's contribution to the team's progress. (For example, "Without keeping your paperwork updated as you did, our team would not have had its report in on time.")
2. Thanking a person for how he or she has contributed to your growth. (For example, "Thanks for your encouragement. It sure made a difference to me.")
3. Speaking in the language of contribution. (For example, "It was thoughtful of you to..." or "I need your help on this projection.")

Encouragement Opportunity 100—*Contribution recognition*

At the next team meeting, make it a point to share with each teammate how he or she has contributed to the effort, improvement, progress and success of the team. List your teammates' names and their contributions below.

____

____

____

____

____

____

Encouragement Opportunity 101—*Recognizing your own contributions to the team*

What were some of your own contributions to the team's efforts, improvement, progress and success?

____

____

____

____

Key Points on Contribution-Recognition Skills

1. Every person needs to feel that the world is a little better because he or she is in it. By recognizing contribution, you fulfill that vital need.
2. Point out every contribution.

BEST TEAM SKILL #48—*EVALUATING-ACTION SKILLS*

Evaluating-action skills are the skills to objectively evaluate the actions taken.

Encouragement Opportunity 102—*Evaluating actions*

Ask your team the following questions after taking actions:

1. What was our goal? ______________________________

____

____

2. What actions have we taken? ______________________________

____

____

3. What results did we achieve? ______________________________

____

____

4. What did we learn? ______________________________

____

____

5. What worked? ______________________________

____

____

6. What didn't work? ______________________________

____

____

7. Where are we now in relationship to our goal? __________

____

____

8. What will be our best action to take? ____________________

____

____

Key Points on Evaluating-Action Skills

1. What worked? What didn't?
2. Where are we now? Where do we want to be? What is our best way of getting there?

BEST TEAM SKILL #49—*CREDIT-SHARING SKILLS*

Credit-sharing skills are the skills of giving or sharing credit, rather than taking credit, for an idea or achievement.

Encouragement Opportunity 103—*Giving credit for all ideas*

Giving credit for all ideas, whether you judge them as usable or not, ensures that your teammates will continue to offer ideas. And the success of your team is based on better ideas. Here are suggested ways to handle new ideas:

1. "Thanks for sharing that idea. The team appreciates your extra effort to improve things around here."
2. "Let's consider whether Joan's idea can be used and, if so, how we can use it."
3. "Again, Joan, thank you. Keep thinking up new and better ways. I hope the rest of the team does the same."

Encouragement Opportunity 104—*Giving credit for achievements*

One of the single most important things the team can do is to obsessively give credit to people for their effort, improvement, progress and success. The more stable a person is, the less he or she needs to wallow in credit and the more he or she can shine the spotlight on others. A person who is secure does not need constant recognition. Giving credit keeps the whole team motivated. The more encouraged the team is, the more successful the team will become—and the more successful you will become!

Key Points on Credit-Sharing Skills

1. Give credit for all ideas, not just the good ones.
2. Let everyone on the team know that they will get credit for their contributions.
3. Be obsessed with giving and sharing credit instead of taking it!

BEST TEAM SKILL #50—*CELEBRATION SKILLS*

Celebration skills involve rewarding and thanking each other after achieving the goal.

Encouragement Opportunity 105—*Celebrating the team*

When celebrating, honor team as well as individual excellence.

Encouragement Opportunity 106—*Reviewing the mutual encouragement process*

To achieve our success, we lived the seven principles of mutual encouragement:

1. THE SYNERGY PRINCIPLE—
   "All of Us Together Can Do More Than Each of Us Can Do Alone"
2. THE COOPERATION PRINCIPLE—
   "Competing Divides Us; Cooperating Multiples Us"
3. THE FOCUS PRINCIPLE—
   "Determining Our Destination Determines Our Destiny"
4. THE RESPECT PRINCIPLE—
   "Centering on Each Other's Strengths Builds Our Force"
5. THE REALITY PRINCIPLE—
   "Accepting 'What Is' Is Our Only Real Starting Point"
6. THE OPTIMISM PRINCIPLE—
   "Believing Problems Have Solutions Gives Us the Advantage"
7. THE PROGRESS PRINCIPLE—
   "Encouraging Progress Precedes Praising Success"

Key Points on Celebrating-Success Skills

1. Celebrate the victory. Include everyone.
2. Savor your team's success! You are one of the rare people in the world who has found a group of people who have made a commitment to work together and succeed together! And so are your teammates. Savor your team's success!

TEAMWORK MAKES THE DREAM WORK

Philosopher Buckminster Fuller spoke of the importance of individual effort in building a better world. Fuller observed, "There are no passengers on the Spaceship Earth. We are all crew!" This is true of any team, family or group in which we find ourselves. We are part of something bigger. The results we achieve together will be for better or for worse, based upon each crew member's encouraging contribution. When every crew member makes a commitment to bring out the best in others, it brings our whole team closer to the dream.

Crew members, all being human, will slip along the way. If each encourager makes a commitment to bring in the out and pick up the down by reaffirming the fifty skills presented here, the team will be back on course. Make sure each new teammate is ready and willing to encourage the others by helping them see that encouragement is part of their responsibility. You can help them by encouraging them to acquire the skills of mutual encouragement.